W9-BBZ-599

# THE HUMAN PATH ACROSS THE CONTINENTS

# PATHWAYS THROUGH ASIA

## Mary Auld

# CRABTREE
PUBLISHING COMPANY
WWW.CRABTREEBOOKS.COM

# CRABTREE
## PUBLISHING COMPANY
### WWW.CRABTREEBOOKS.COM

**Author:** Mary Auld

**Editorial director:** Kathy Middleton

**Editors:** Rachel Cooke, Janine Deschenes

**Design:** Jeni Child

**Photo research:** FFP Consulting; Tammy McGarr

**Proofreader:** Melissa Boyce

**Print and production coordinator:** Katherine Berti

Produced for Crabtree Publishing Company by
FFP Consulting Limited

**Images**
t=Top, b=Bottom, tl=Top Left, tr=Top Right, bl=Bottom Left, br=Bottom
Right, c=Center, lc=Left Center, rc=Right Center

**Alamy**
T0KGCE: p. 6; Pascal Mannaerts: p. 25t
**Getty**
The India Today Group: p. 23lc
**iStock**
NeoPhoto: p. 8b; LeoPatrizi: p. 9t; shilh: p. 12b; zhaojiankang: p. 13t
**Shutterstock**
IRIT3530: TOC; chetansoni: p. 5; Irina Kononova: p. 7t; DiegoMariottini: p.
9rc; Francesco Dazzi: p. 11br; BartlomiejMagierowski: p. 15lc; Phuong D.
Nguyen: p. 16b; Phuong D. Nguyen: p. 17t; Akhmad Dody Firmansyah: p.
19lc; GeorginaCaptures: p. 19br; pendakisolo: p. 21tr; Constantin Stanciu:
p. 21lc; Gritsana P: p. 23tr; MehmetO: p. 24t; Emily Marie Wilson: p. 25rc;
Rob Crandall: p. 26rc; S-F: p. 27t; YusufAslan: p. 29t; Photo Oz: p. 29b

**All other images from Shutterstock**

**Maps:** Jeni Child

**Library and Archives Canada Cataloguing in Publication**

Title: Pathways through Asia / Mary Auld.
Names: Auld, Mary, author.
Description: Series statement: The human path across the continents |
  Includes index.
Identifiers: Canadiana (print) 20190112042 |
  Canadiana (ebook) 20190112050 |
  ISBN 9780778766018 (hardcover) |
  ISBN 9780778766469 (softcover) |
  ISBN 9781427123985 (HTML)
Subjects: LCSH: Human ecology—Asia—Juvenile literature. |
  LCSH: Asia—Juvenile literature.
Classification: LCC GF651 .A95 2019 | DDC j304.2095—dc23

**Library of Congress Cataloging-in-Publication Data**

CIP available at the Library of Congress

LCCN 2019030382

## Crabtree Publishing Company
www.crabtreebooks.com       1-800-387-7650

Printed in the U.S.A./082019/CG20190712

**Published in Canada**
**Crabtree Publishing**
616 Welland Ave.
St. Catharines, Ontario
L2M 5V6

**Published in the United States**
**Crabtree Publishing**
PMB 59051
350 Fifth Avenue, 59th Floor
New York, New York 10118

**Published in the United Kingdom**
**Crabtree Publishing**
Maritime House
Basin Road North, Hove
BN41 1WR

**Published in Australia**
**Crabtree Publishing**
Unit 3–5 Currumbin Court
Capalaba
QLD 4157

# CONTENTS

## ASIA

# The Human Path
# ACROSS ASIA

Tokyo skyline

Welcome to Asia, the world's largest continent. Asia is a giant region, covering 30 percent of Earth's land area. It also includes most of the world's biggest country, Russia. With more than 4.5 billion people, out of the 7.5 billion people living on Earth, Asia also has the highest population of any continent.

▼ **ASIA'S AMAZING LANDSCAPES** range from snowy, northern forests in Russia to the tropical rain forests of Indonesia. There are hot, dry deserts in Saudi Arabia and Iran, and huge grasslands in Kazakhstan and Mongolia. Lying between India and China are the Himalayas, the world's highest mountains.

The people of Asia are equally diverse. The 48 countries within the continent include some of the world's oldest cultures. Asia is where the world's leading religions began, including **Buddhism, Christianity**, and **Islam**. Traditionally, many journeys within Asia were **pilgrimages** to visit religious **shrines**, such as Mecca in Saudi Arabia or the Ganges River in India.

▲ **CITIES IN ASIA** have grown dramatically over the last 50 years. In 1970, most Asians lived in villages in the country, working as farmers. Today, half the population lives in large, modern cities. They have jobs in **industries**, making goods to be sold around the world. Out of the 33 **megacities** in the world, 20 are in Asia, including Tokyo in Japan and Delhi in India. Many of these cities have grown so quickly they have become overcrowded. Getting around can be difficult. Many cities in Asia are trying to make travel quicker and easier by creating new transportation systems, such as subways and bicycle rental stations.

Waterfalls, China·Vietnam border

## Map of Asia

RUSSIA

GEORGIA
KAZAKHSTAN
MONGOLIA
NORTH KOREA
SOUTH KOREA
JAPAN

Black Sea
Caspian Sea
TURKEY
ARMENIA
AZERBAIJAN
UZBEKISTAN
KYRGYZSTAN
TURKMENISTAN
TAJIKISTAN

LEBANON
SYRIA
ISRAEL
JORDAN
IRAQ
IRAN
AFGHANISTAN
CHINA

KUWAIT
PAKISTAN
BAHRAIN
QATAR
NEPAL
BHUTAN
BANGLADESH
TAIWAN
PACIFIC OCEAN

SAUDI ARABIA
UNITED ARAB EMIRATES
OMAN
Arabian Sea
INDIA
MYANMAR

YEMEN
INDIAN OCEAN
LAOS
THAILAND
CAMBODIA
VIETNAM
PHILIPPINES

SRI LANKA
MALAYSIA
BRUNEI
SINGAPORE

EUROPE
ASIA

INDONESIA
PAPUA NEW GUINEA

▶ **PEOPLE HAVE TRAVELED** across Asia to buy and sell goods for thousands of years. They created **trade** routes, such as the Silk Road from China, across Central Asia to Europe. Today, journeys for trade continue. Most goods are now moved by ships, trucks, and aircraft, although some people still use animals.

The fast pace of change in Asia has created a mix of ancient cultures and the latest technology. Many people in Asia have quickly become rich thanks to international trade and free markets. Other people still live in great **poverty**. The journeys we will take in this book will help us understand the geography of this amazing continent—and explain why people live where they do.

Mule moving air-conditioning unit, India

# Across ASIA by Train

**RUSSIA**

URAL MOUNTAINS

Moscow

Yekaterinburg

Omsk

**KAZAKHSTAN**

The Trans-Siberian Railway is the longest railway in the world. You can board a train at Moscow for a 5,772-mile (9,289 km) journey across the **Eurasian landmass** to Vladivostok on the Pacific Ocean. Moscow, the capital of Russia, is in Europe. But after crossing the Ural Mountains, the train enters Asia—with 4,660 miles (7,500 km) still to go across Siberia.

### ⬇ THE TRANS-SIBERIAN RAILWAY

was completed in 1916. With few major highways in the huge area of Siberia, this rail link is still vital. The Trans-Siberian is the busiest rail track in the world. Trains pass each other every five minutes. It is used for transporting both goods and millions of passengers each year. Tourists travel alongside Russian families and business people. Some people are traveling long distance, others are making local trips. A train from Moscow to Vladivostok takes about six and a half days. It passes through seven **time zones**.

A Trans-Siberian train

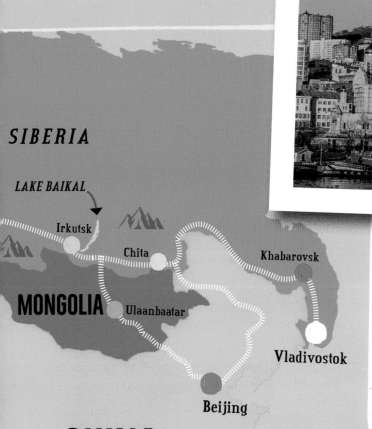

SIBERIA

LAKE BAIKAL

Irkutsk

Chita

Khabarovsk

MONGOLIA

Ulaanbaatar

Vladivostok

Beijing

CHINA

Rail routes

The port at Vladivostok

▲ **VLADIVOSTOK** is the end of the rail line. This large city earns money from the fishing industry and from trade through its **port** on the Pacific Ocean. You can continue your journey from there by ferry to Japan or South Korea, or fly home.

Apart from the Vladivostok route, there are two other routes on the Trans-Siberian. Both end up in Beijing, China. One travels through Mongolia, the other though Manchuria, a region of China.

Village by Lake Baikal

➡ **IT TAKES DAYS** for the train to cross the Eurasian **Steppe**, which stretches across the continent. The steppe is made up of open plains and birchwood forests that are covered in snow in winter. Although there are scattered towns and villages, few people have settled in Siberia. The extreme winter cold and the **remoteness** of Siberia make life there incredibly hard. People who do live in Siberia make a living from mining and forestry.

Lake Baikal lies a little over halfway across the steppe. It is the largest and deepest freshwater lake in the world. There is spectacular mountain scenery along this section of the route. From there, the train follows mountain passes north of Mongolia, before rejoining flatter land along the Chinese border.

**PEOPLE**

**ALONG THE WAY**

Batuhan is a Mongolian clothes trader. He travels to Moscow along the Trans-Siberian Railway to buy clothes. He then sells the latest Russian fashions to people at the stations as he travels back home by train. People crowd around his railcar at each stop, attracted by the clothes he displays from its window.

# A Bike Tour of
# SEOUL

MONGOLIA

CHINA

NORTH KOREA

*SEA OF JAPAN*

SEOUL

SOUTH KOREA

JAPAN

Bike route
Seoul

*Han River*

Jongno

Yongsan

Seocho

Seoul, the capital of South Korea, is an ancient city that first grew up because of its position on the Han River. This made it a good place for trading with China. Today, Seoul has become one of Asia's richest cities, particularly because of its electronics industries. You can rent a city bike to explore Seoul's mix of old and new buildings.

**▼ THE JONGNO DISTRICT** is where we start our bicycle ride. Jongno is home to many beautiful palaces, **historic monuments**, and religious shrines. These were built by the kings of Korea hundreds of years ago. Nearby are traditional wooden houses, or *hanoks*. Some of them have been turned into guesthouses to welcome tourists.

From Jongno we cycle into Yongsan, a more modern area. After being nearly destroyed in the Korean War (1950–1953), Seoul grew rapidly in the 1970s and 1980s. South Korea became famous for making electronic goods such as televisions, music systems, computers, and cell phones. With many of these industries located in Seoul, the city's population exploded. Now, 10 million people live there—nearly one Korean in every five.

Old palace in the center of Seoul

Seoul Bike rental station

### THE HEADQUARTERS OF SAMSUNG

lie in Seocho District, a cycle ride across the Han River. Samsung is the world's largest maker of smartphones, and South Korea's best-known company. This area is also known as Samsung Town. More than 320,000 people work for Samsung worldwide, and the company makes 20 percent of South Korea's **exports**. Like several other large companies in South Korea, Samsung has given bicycles to the Seoul Bike rental system.

### SEOUL BIKE,

the city's public bicycle rental system, was started in 2015. It already has more than 30,000 bikes available to rent. Users reserve and pay for their bike rentals by using a smartphone app.

Seoul Bike is one way in which the city's government is trying to reduce air pollution and traffic jams. Seoul's population grew so quickly that the roads were unable to cope with so many cars. The city has created new subway lines, bus lanes, and car-sharing systems. Technology is used to reduce traffic congestion. For example, public transportation users pay by smart cards, and **GPS** technology is used to manage bus movements. Car sharing also works through smartphones.

Samsung's headquarters

## Pause for
## REFLECTION

- How do you think South Korea's success in technology has affected the lives of its people?
- How does technology help manage transportation systems?
- What benefits would a bike rental system bring to a city like Seoul?

# A Pilgrimage in JAPAN

The islands that make up Japan lie in the Pacific Ocean, to the east of the Asian mainland. Most of Japan's 127 million people live in modern cities, such as Tokyo, the capital, and Osaka. However, the Japanese have built religious shrines far from cities. They traditionally valued nature's beauty. Today, many people still walk to these places as **pilgrims**.

↓ **THE KUMANO KODO** pilgrimage routes are found in the beautiful forests of the Kii Mountains to the south of Osaka. People walk the network of paths to visit **sacred** sites, some of which date back more than 1,200 years. These sites have temples and shrines that were created by Japanese Buddhists. Buddhism began in Asia. Travelers from India shared Buddhist ideas across Asia, reaching Japan in the sixth century.

CHINA

RUSSIA

PACIFIC OCEAN

SEA OF JAPAN

NORTH KOREA

SOUTH KOREA

JAPAN

Osaka

Tokyo

Koyasan

Yoshino and Omine

Kii Mountains

Tanabe

Kumano Sanzan

—— Pilgrim routes

Kumano Kodo walker

**↑ TO WALK THE PILGRIM ROUTES** today, people usually travel by train from Osaka to the city of Tanabe on the coast. From there, they continue their journeys into the mountains by bus, reaching the Kumano Kodo routes. In the past, people took weeks to walk the trails, but few visitors today can take that time away from work. By using connecting buses, most are able to see many of the shrines scattered throughout the mountains in four or five days.

**↓ SETTLEMENTS** have grown up around the larger shrines over the centuries. They were formed by religious communities of Buddhist **monks**. They also provide places for pilgrims to stay. The most important shrines are Yoshino and Omine, Kumano Sanzan, and Koyasan. These three places, along with 191 miles (307 km) of the pilgrimage paths, are now recognized as a **World Heritage Site**.

Today, more than 15 million people a year come to the area. Some visit as pilgrims, but many simply as tourists. The region has set up its own tourist network to help guide tourists and to protect the people and nature in the area. It offers travel information, including maps, and suggests places to stay. It encourages both visitors and locals to try to respect the nature that surrounds them, for example, by keeping it clean of trash.

Kumano Nachi Taisha shrine, Kumano Sanzan

Monk in Koyasan

**PEOPLE**

**ALONG THE WAY**

Dan is a Buddhist monk at one of the temples of Koyasan. He helps run the guesthouse his temple offers to visitors. Many Buddhists do not eat meat, so Dan helps prepare vegetarian food for his guests. The money that visitors pay for their stay helps cover the costs for the temple's upkeep. Dan is happy to share his faith, leading guests in morning prayers.

# High-Speed Train
# THROUGH CHINA

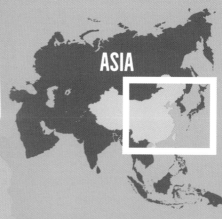

**ASIA**

MONGOLIA

|||||||| Rail routes
||||||||
||||||||

Beijing

NORTH KOREA

SOUTH KOREA

**CHINA**

Shanghai

BHUTAN

INDIA

Kunming

MYANMAR

BANGLADESH

VIETNAM

LAOS

TAIWAN

Hong Kong

Since the **1980**s, China has been changing very quickly. It has many new, modern industries. This has helped it become a much richer country. Transportation has also changed rapidly. In just **10** years, China has built the world's biggest high-speed rail network. With over **18,000** miles (**29,000** km) of track laid since **2008**, China has more high-speed railroads than all other countries in the world put together.

A Fuxinghao train passes a new development

◀ **IN BEIJING,** China's capital, you can board a Fuxinghao train, one of the world's fastest passenger trains. It travels at an average speed of about 217 miles per hour (350 kph). In just four and a half hours, it can take you to Shanghai, the heart of China's **economy**, 819 miles (1,318 km) away. The train passes through many new cities. People have moved to these cities to work in giant factories, which make goods for export around the world.

Building a new rail network so quickly has created many jobs in construction. It has also helped China develop its own train-making industry. High-speed train travel has a positive benefit for the environment too. Airlines have stopped flying between cities that are linked by cheaper and more reliable trains. This means less pollution.

Lei Miao lives in a tiny apartment in Shanghai. She moved to the city to work for an electronics company. Until recently, Lei was able to return to her home village in the mountains of Yunnan province just once every two years. Now with a new, fast train line to Kunming, she is able to see her parents several times a year.

## ⬆ TENS OF MILLIONS OF CHINESE

Crowds at Shanghai station

people have moved from villages to cities to work. The high-speed train network has changed their lives. Before it was built, returning to see their families in villages would take many days' travel. For some, it was nearly impossible. Now, the new rail lines mean a journey takes just a few hours.

## ⬇ CHINA'S RAILROADS are still developing. New

lines, such as a connection to Hong Kong, continue to open. In Shanghai, you can travel to the airport on a futuristic Maglev train. This train has no wheels and uses magnets to float at speeds of up to 250 miles per hour (400 kph). Maglev trains are quieter and faster than ordinary trains. Meanwhile, China is using its new technical knowledge to build railways in other parts of the world, such as Africa.

Maglev train, Shanghai

# Shipping Out From HONG KONG

British settlement, Hong Kong, illustration from 1840

Hong Kong is one of the world's largest ports. For a long time, this **peninsula** and island city has also been the gateway to China—and a way for China to connect with the rest of the world. The busy harbor is packed with **container** ships. They bring goods from all over the world to China. Then they load exports from China to be shipped to the rest of the world.

HONG KONG

**↑ A DEEPWATER HARBOR,** protected by high hills all around, helped Hong Kong to grow into a major settlement. The Chinese name "Hong Kong" means "fragrant harbor." It was a trading port under Chinese rule. Then, in the nineteenth century, the British took over Hong Kong. They turned it into a military and trading base.

Starting from just a few thousand, Hong Kong's population grew rapidly during British rule as people moved there to find jobs. Today, Hong Kong is home to nearly 7.5 million people. It is now part of China once more. The steep hills around the harbor mean there is a shortage of land for building, so people live in tall skyscrapers.

View of Victoria Harbour, Hong Kong

Shenzhen

**HONG KONG**

Victoria Harbour

Hong Kong Island

Shipping route

**FACTORIES IN SHENZHEN** make many of the goods shipped out of Hong Kong's port. This new city is on the Chinese mainland next door to Hong Kong. In just a few years, Shenzhen has become the electronics "capital" of the world. People have moved from small villages all over China to work in its factories. This has made Shenzhen a giant modern city of 12 million people. Televisions, cell phones, and all kinds of household electrical products are made there.

Electronics factory, Shenzhen

Containers at Hong Kong's port

**SHIPPING CONTAINERS** arrive in Hong Kong from Shenzhen by truck. At the harbor, giant cranes load these containers onto huge ships. An amazing 19.6 million containers pass through the port every year. Over 300 ships a week sail out of Hong Kong, headed for 450 other ports around the world. Some travel east across the Pacific Ocean to the Americas. Others move west to Africa and Europe.

## Pause for REFLECTION

- How do you think Hong Kong's harbor has helped China's industries grow? How has it contributed to Shenzhen's success?
- Why do you think people choose to live in Hong Kong's skyscrapers?

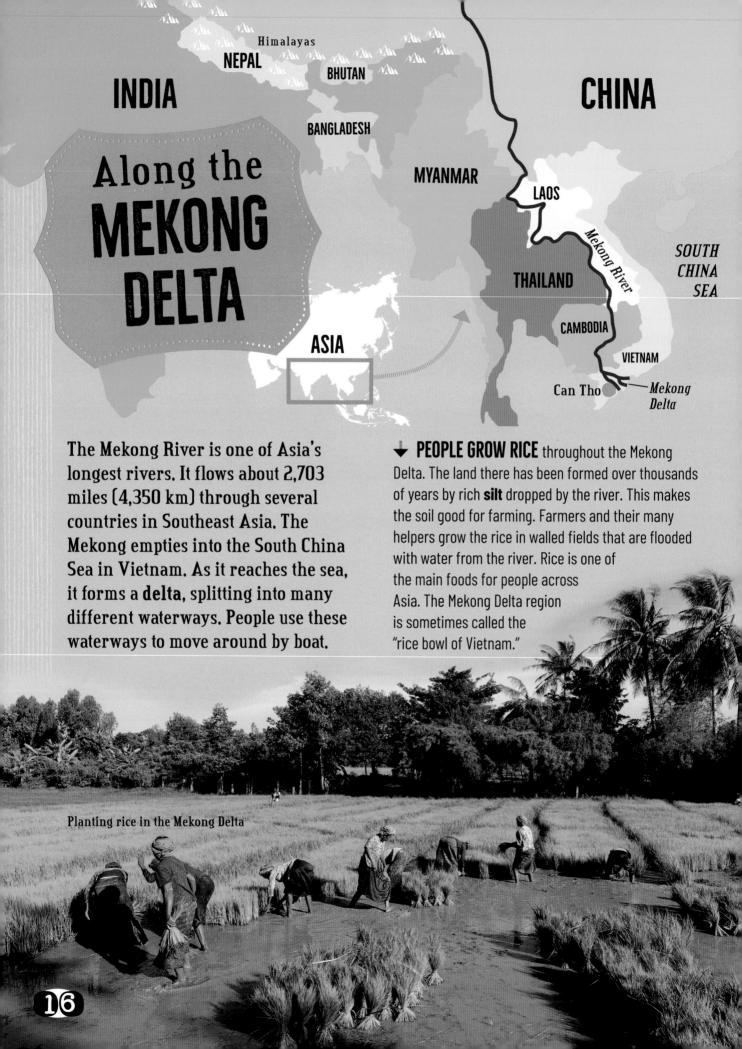

# Along the MEKONG DELTA

**INDIA**

Himalayas
**NEPAL**
**BHUTAN**
**BANGLADESH**

**MYANMAR**

**CHINA**

**LAOS**

Mekong River

**THAILAND**

**SOUTH CHINA SEA**

**CAMBODIA**

**VIETNAM**

Can Tho

Mekong Delta

**ASIA**

The Mekong River is one of Asia's longest rivers. It flows about 2,703 miles (4,350 km) through several countries in Southeast Asia. The Mekong empties into the South China Sea in Vietnam. As it reaches the sea, it forms a **delta**, splitting into many different waterways. People use these waterways to move around by boat.

↓ **PEOPLE GROW RICE** throughout the Mekong Delta. The land there has been formed over thousands of years by rich **silt** dropped by the river. This makes the soil good for farming. Farmers and their many helpers grow the rice in walled fields that are flooded with water from the river. Rice is one of the main foods for people across Asia. The Mekong Delta region is sometimes called the "rice bowl of Vietnam."

Planting rice in the Mekong Delta

**SETTLEMENTS** in the Mekong Delta formed around farms and markets where people sold their crops. Today, more than 20 million people live in the region. Many still meet in floating markets to sell their produce. Some small settlements can only be reached by boat, but others have grown into towns and cities. They are connected by road and river.

The city of Can Tho has a population of around 1.5 million. Originally built as a fort for soldiers, it is now an important economic center, with a large river port and airport. These transportation links allow farmers to export their produce around the world.

Floating market near Can Tho

**BETWEEN AUGUST** and November each year, **monsoon** rains cause regular flooding in the Mekong Delta. People build their houses on stilts to allow for the changing water levels caused by the floods. Other houses are actually boats that float on the water. Much of the delta's land is low lying and close to the sea. However, sea levels are rising as a result of **climate change**. Some of the delta's farmland may soon be permanently flooded. The soil in other areas will become saltier from seawater, making it hard to farm. One plan for the future is to plant new areas of forest along the coast. These forest areas will protect farmland from the salt water.

## PEOPLE ALONG THE WAY

Linh lives in a village in the Mekong Delta. She works for the local rice farm. Her family also has a small plot of land where they grow fruits and vegetables. Once a week, Linh takes their produce to a floating market near Can Tho. The journey takes two hours, but her family needs the extra money she makes.

Houses on stilts near Can Tho

# Getting to Work in JAKARTA

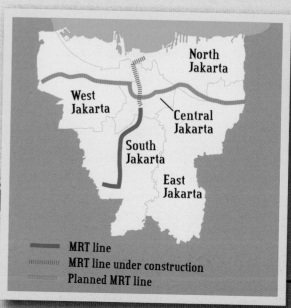

Central Jakarta and its suburbs

The country of Indonesia is made up of many islands off the coast of Southeast Asia. Its capital city, Jakarta, lies on the island of Java. Jakarta is a stopping point for ships traveling around Asia. This has made it an important commercial center. Many people have moved to Jakarta to work, so the city has grown very quickly and now spreads over a large area. Journeys to and from work can be long and difficult.

▲ **GREATER JAKARTA** is now one of the world's largest megacities, second only to Tokyo, Japan. It has a population of more than 30 million people. The original area of the city, Central Jakarta, is where the banks and offices are found. Businesses have built huge skyscrapers to make the most of the expensive land in this area.

People mainly live outside the central area. Jakarta lies on flat ground, next to the sea. Outside its center, there is plenty of land to build on, so the city's suburbs have spread outward with low-rise housing. This includes very poor areas, where people have built their own makeshift houses. Jakarta's huge population puts pressure on supplies of clean water. The city is working to improve the water pipelines, particularly to areas of poorer housing.

MYANMAR

LAOS

THAILAND

CAMBODIA

VIETNAM

PHILIPPINES

BRUNEI

MALAYSIA

SINGAPORE

INDONESIA

Jakarta    JAVA

North Jakarta

West Jakarta

Central Jakarta

South Jakarta

East Jakarta

— MRT line

▨▨ MRT line under construction

Planned MRT line

Motorcycles, Jakarta

**↑ HEAVY TRAFFIC** is a problem in Jakarta. Many people have to travel each day for work from the outer areas of Greater Jakarta to its central district. As a result, many of them choose to travel by motorcycle as these can cut through the traffic. They are also cheaper to buy and run than a car. However, riding motorcycles on busy roads is dangerous, and there are many accidents. So there are now car-sharing systems, organized through smartphone apps, to help cut down on traffic.

**↓ PUBLIC TRANSPORTATION** in Jakarta is not available to many of its residents. The Jakarta city government is trying to improve this situation with better bus lanes and new trains. In 2019, an MRT (mass rapid transit) system opened with a 10-mile (16 km) line between Central and South Jakarta. The trains running on this line are nicknamed *Rantagga*, which means "war chariot" in Javanese, the local language. Better public transportation and traffic management will help cut down pollution from cars and improve air quality in the city.

Travelers on the new MRT

## Pause for
## REFLECTION

- Why do you think Jakarta's flat surroundings have meant that the city has spread outward?
- What are the advantages and disadvantages of using motorcycles in a city?
- Why is it important that a city has good public transportation links?

Hikers below Mount Everest

# Trekking in the
# HIMALAYAS

The Himalayan mountain range is the highest in the world. It is sometimes called "The Roof of the World." The country of Nepal lies to the southern edge of the Himalayas. People from all over the world come to walk along its high trails or to climb its great peaks, including Mount Everest.

⬆ **MOUNT EVEREST,** at 29,029 feet (8,848 m), is the tallest peak in the world. It lies on the border between Nepal and China. Eight out of the world's 10 highest mountains are found in the Himalayas in Nepal. The range lies where two **tectonic plates** meet. These slow-moving plates form the outer layer of Earth. The plates push against each other, which has caused the land to fold up and form the Himalayas. The plates are still pushing together, so the mountain range is slowly getting higher. This movement also creates a risk of earthquakes. There was a major earthquake in Nepal in 2015.

ASIA

PAKISTAN

CHINA

*Himalayas*

Cho Oyu (26,864 ft/8,188 m)
Mount Everest (29,029 ft/8,848 m)
Makalu (27,838 ft/8,485 m)

The high peaks of the Himalayas

INDIA

NEPAL

Kathmandu

BHUTAN

Dhaulagiri I (26,795 ft/8,167 m)
Annapurna (26,545 ft/8,091 m)
Manaslu (26,781 ft/8,163 m)

Lhotse (27,940 ft/8,516 m)
Kangchenjunga (28,169 ft/8,586 m)

BANGLADESH

MYANMAR

Sherpas carrying baggage

**KATHMANDU** is the capital of Nepal. It lies on flatter land below the Himalayas. It grew up as a center of trade between China and India, and also as a market for the farming communities that surround it. Both **Hindu** and Buddhist people live in Kathmandu. It has many religious temples and seven World Heritage Sites. It is sometimes called "the City of Temples."

The 2015 earthquake badly damaged the city and it is still being rebuilt. Like the rest of Nepal today, Kathmandu's economy is focused on tourism. Most visitors arrive at its airport and visit its temple sites. Walkers and climbers then travel to the mountains by bus or plane.

Street in Kathmandu

## NETWORKS OF TREKKING TRAILS are focused around different mountain areas, such as Mount Everest or Annapurna. A trek may take a few days or several weeks. An **expedition** to climb Everest will take around two months. Treks take place mainly in protected **reserves**.

Sherpas are an **ethnic group** of Nepal who mainly live in the mountains. They have farmed there for many centuries. This gives them excellent knowledge of the mountain trails. Many Sherpas work guiding visitors and carrying their baggage. Their families may run simple guesthouses, built in their small mountain villages.

### PEOPLE ALONG THE WAY

Some Sherpas are expert mountaineers. Brothers Mingma and Changg Dawa Sherpa have climbed all of Nepal's eight highest mountains. Using their skills and local knowledge, they have set up a business in Nepal that organizes climbing expeditions. Climbers from around the world join them to climb these peaks.

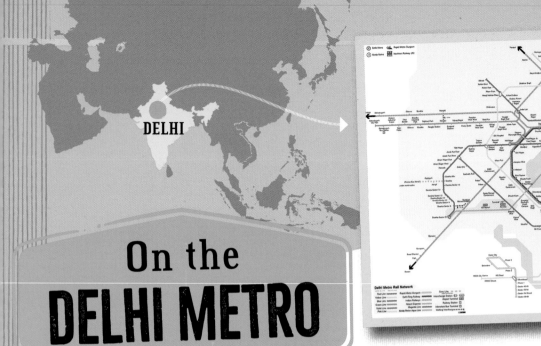

DELHI

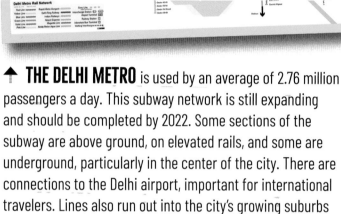

# On the
# DELHI METRO

Like many Asian cities, Delhi has grown rapidly. It is now the third-largest urban area in the world. New Delhi, a district of Delhi and India's capital, is located at the center of Delhi. Traffic congestion is a big problem there. Since 2002, however, the Delhi Metro has made a huge difference to the quality of life in this busy city.

**The Red Fort**

▲ **THE DELHI METRO** is used by an average of 2.76 million passengers a day. This subway network is still expanding and should be completed by 2022. Some sections of the subway are above ground, on elevated rails, and some are underground, particularly in the center of the city. There are connections to the Delhi airport, important for international travelers. Lines also run out into the city's growing suburbs for use by its many **commuters**.

▼ **DELHI** is an old settlement and has been an important political center for many centuries. At the Chandni Chowk station on the Yellow Line, you can visit the Red Fort. Built in the seventeenth century, this red-stone fortress was home to India's rulers for nearly 200 years. Today, it houses several museums.

**Yellow Line of the Delhi Metro**

▶ **AS A MODERN** subway system, the Delhi Metro has been planned with environmental concerns in mind. In 2011, it was the first city subway to be recognized by the United Nations for its work on reducing the gases that contribute to climate change. For example, its trains use less of the fuel that creates these gases—instead, the trains' brakes make extra electricity when they are used. This extra electricity helps to power the trains.

Artists, with the input of local communities such as school children, have decorated the subway stations. The art celebrates different aspects of Delhi's culture and Indian animals, including those used for transportation in the past.

**Subway station artwork based on children's drawings**

### Pause for
### REFLECTION

- Why do you think the Delhi Metro's builders encouraged local people to be involved in decorating the stations?
- How would you decorate a subway or rail station close to your home?
- How has Delhi's subway been planned to have a smaller environmental impact? Why is this important?

**City of Noida**

▶ **THE SUBWAY CONNECTS** central Delhi with its growing outer areas, such as Noida on the subway's Blue Line. Noida is a new city, planned from the beginning to mix high-rise housing with trees and park areas in between. It attracts people looking for good homes close to the city and transportation links.

# Ride With Nomads in IRAN

IRAN

Qashqai territory ........
Migration routes ▬▬▬
Summer grazing
Winter grazing

ZAGROS MOUNTAINS

Shiraz

PERSIAN GULF

Qashqai girl with a herd

Many people in Asia still live in the countryside, farming the land or raising animals. A few of these people are **nomads**. Nomads move with the seasons in search of land with a lot of grass for their animals to eat. One nomadic group of people are the Qashqai, who live around the Zagros Mountains of Iran.

▲ **THE QASHQAI PEOPLE** live in small communities, keeping herds of goats and sheep. These animals graze on grass and other plants over large areas of land. Every summer, each community moves to the high mountains so their herds can feed on the plants that grow there. In fall, they return with their animals to lower fields, away from the mountains' cold winter weather and snow. Some groups travel around 300 miles (480 km) each year, from the mountains near Shiraz to the flatter land closer to the Persian Gulf. They walk or ride on donkeys alongside their herds. When they stop, they make temporary villages with their tents.

**THE QASHQAI DEPEND ON HERDS** for food and wool. The women prepare the wool by hand for weaving. They use wild plants to make the dyes they use to color the wool. They use the wool to make clothes, carpets for their tents, and bags to transport their belongings on their annual **migration**. Today, they also sell much of what they make.

Preparing wool for weaving

**SOFT WOOL** from the Qashqai is very good quality. People around the world buy Qashqai rugs and bags. Traders visit Qashqai settlements to buy their goods. Each item is unique, designed by its makers using traditional patterns.

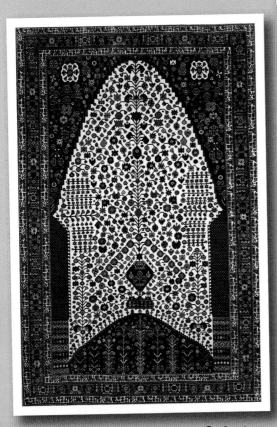

Qashqai rug

Qashqai washing carpets in a stream

**PEOPLE ALONG THE WAY**

Shima is a young Qashqai woman. She is working with her community to open up their tented summer village in the mountains to tourists. Visitors eat Qashqai food, listen to their music, and sleep in their tents. Shima likes to show them the carpets she is making. Shima hopes the money the tourists bring will help protect the Qashqai's nomadic way of life.

**LIFE AS A NOMAD** is very hard. Many younger Qashqai choose to settle permanently in cities such as Shiraz, where they can find work. Growing towns and cities have taken some of the Qashqai's lower grazing land. New roads cross their migration routes, placing their herds in danger. Community leaders are working to protect their traditional grazing lands. For example, they are developing **ecotourism**.

EUROPE   ASIA

Port Rashid — Airport

PERSIAN GULF

Dubai Mall

UNITED ARAB EMIRATES

DUBAI

Burj Khalifa

DESERT

# Walk Around the DUBAI MALL

The city of Dubai lies on the Persian Gulf. It is part of the United Arab Emirates (UAE), a country that has become rich from oil production. However, Dubai has less oil than other parts of the UAE. Instead, the city has built its wealth as a center for business, travel, and shopping. A walk around the Dubai Mall will take you several hours. It is one of the largest shopping centers in the world.

Construction workers, Dubai

**↓ DUBAI BEGAN** as a fishing village in the eighteenth century. Helped by its port, it grew into an important trade center. In the 1960s, Dubai's rulers realized its position in West Asia made it a perfect stopping point for flights between Europe, Southeast Asia, and Australia. They developed its airport to attract passenger planes. This also brought in international businesses. Dubai quickly became a large, rich, high-rise city. Today, it includes the world's tallest building, the Burj Khalifa. Opened in 2010, it is 2717 feet (828 m) high.

**↑ TO BUILD AND MAINTAIN** the city, Dubai needed workers from outside the country. In the past 25 years, Dubai's population has grown from just under 700,000 to nearly 3 million. Most of this increase has come through **migration**, particularly from India and Pakistan. Many new migrants work in construction, but others work in Dubai's banks, shops, and other service industries.

The Burj Khalifa tops the Dubai skyline

The Dubai Mall aquarium

▲ **TOURISTS ARE DRAWN** to Dubai for its spectacular skyline, hot desert weather, and its shopping opportunities. Opened in 2008, the Dubai Mall is the largest of its shopping centers. It offers more than 1,300 different stores, with more than 200 places to eat and drink. Other attractions include an Olympic-size ice rink, a multiscreen cinema, and the Dubai Aquarium and Underwater Zoo. The mall's overall floor space is 5.9 million square feet (548,128 square m).

## Pause for
# REFLECTION

- What effect do you think Dubai's rapid growth has had on its people's everyday lives?
- What do you think attracts migrants to Dubai?

A Dubai Mall shopper

◀ **MORE THAN 80 MILLION PEOPLE** visit the mall each year. Some visitors are from the UAE, but many are from other countries. They may be stopping briefly in Dubai on their way elsewhere, or visiting the city on business or for a vacation. The UAE is a Muslim country. While the mall's stores are international, it also has features that reflect the local religion. For example, Muslims pray at regular times throughout the day, so there are prayer rooms for both men and women on all four levels of the mall.

Hagia Sophia, Istanbul

# Drive Into Europe at
# ISTANBUL

Turkey is a country that lies in both Asia and Europe. The Bosphorus is a strait, or narrow waterway, that forms the border between the two continents. Turkey's largest city, Istanbul, sits on both sides of the strait. This position gives Istanbul good transportation and trade connections. Trucks full of Turkish goods drive from Asia into Europe via Istanbul.

⬆ **ISTANBUL'S POSITION** has made it an important city since ancient times. In the fourth century, it was one of the great cities of the **Roman Empire**, as well as a major center for Christians. However, in the fifteenth century, it was conquered by Turkish Muslims and became the capital of the **Ottoman Empire**. Istanbul's history gives it a mixed cultural heritage. For example, Hagia Sophia is a famous World Heritage Site. Hagia Sophia was first built as a Christian cathedral. It later became a Muslim mosque. Today, it is one of the city's museums.

EUROPE    ASIA

TURKEY

ISTANBUL

BLACK SEA

Yavuz Sultan Selim Bridge

Fatih Sultan Mehmet Bridge

Bosphorus Bridge

Bosphorus

Eurasia Tunnel

SEA OF MARMARA

Highways

Cloth factory, Istanbul

Mehmet drives a truck for a living. He takes clothes made in a factory on the eastern side of Istanbul to stores in Germany. The opening of the Yavuz Sultan Selim Bridge, the third Bosphorus bridge, cut his journey time, bypassing the center of the city. It now takes him less than two days to drive to the big German city of Frankfurt.

## ⬆ THE CLOTHING TRADE

has always been connected to Istanbul. Historically, the city was the western end of the Silk Road trade route that brought cloth across Asia to Europe. Today, Turkey's farmers produce their own cotton and silk. These raw materials are transported to factories in Istanbul where they are turned into cloth. Istanbul also has many factories making clothes from the cloth. Turkey is the sixth-largest exporter of clothes in the world.

## ⬇ TRUCKS EXPORT

many of the clothes made in Istanbul to western Europe. It takes less than two days by road to Germany, for example. Trucks from the Asian side of the city have to cross the Bosphorus. In the past, travelers had to use ferries. But since the 1970s, three new road bridges have been built, the last opening in 2016. There is also a new road tunnel that opened the same year. These new connections helped Istanbul expand, particularly on the Asian side of the city, which was less developed. Industry there has grown with the help of faster and easier transportation to Europe.

Fatih Sultan Mehmet Bridge over the Bosphorus

# GLOSSARY

**Buddhism** A world religion that follows the teaching of the Buddha

**Christianity** A world religion based on the teaching of Jesus Christ

**climate change** Change in climate patterns around the world due to global warming, or the gradual increase in Earth's temperature

**commuters** People who travel regularly from where they live to where they work, which may be some distance away

**container** A large metal box, usually of a standard size, used to transport goods by ship, rail, and truck

**delta** A D-shaped area of flat land, often marshy, where a river or rivers empty into a sea or ocean

**economy** The system by which goods and services are made, sold, bought, and used

**ecotourism** Vacation travel that aims not to leave a bad effect on the environment of the places visited. It often takes place in protected natural areas.

**ethnic group** A group of people who share the same cultural background, or are descended from the same family roots

**Eurasian landmass** The mainland area created by the continents of Europe and Asia joined together

**expedition** A journey of discovery

**exports** Goods sent to be sold in another country

**GPS** Short for Global Positioning System. A navigation system using signals from satellites to make maps.

**Hindu** A person who follows Hinduism—an Indian religion and way of life

**historic monuments** Large, old buildings that are interesting for their history

**industries** Groups of companies that produce goods and services

**Islam** A world religion based on the teachings of the Prophet Muhammed. Its followers are called Muslims.

**megacities** Cities with populations of over 10 million

**migrants** People who live and work outside their country of origin

**migration** To travel to live in a new place

**monks** Men who are part of a religious community

**monsoon** Seasonal winds that blow at a particular time of year, bringing either very wet or dry weather

**nomads** People who have no permanent home but travel from place to place, often with the seasons

**Ottoman Empire** Refers to a Muslim empire that existed in Turkey from the 1300s to 1918

**peninsula** An area of coastal land that is almost completely surrounded by water

**pilgrims** People who make long or difficult journeys, usually for religious reasons

**pilgrimages** Long or difficult journeys made by a pilgrim or group of pilgrims

**port** A place where ships load and unload cargo

**poverty** The state of not having enough money for basic needs, such as food, clothing, and shelter

**remoteness** Being far away from large settlements

**reserves** In Asia, an area of land set aside to protect wildlife, plants, and landscape

**Roman Empire** An empire, centered on the city of Rome, that ruled large parts of Europe around 2,000 years ago

**sacred** Describes something connected with, and important to, a religion

**shrines** Holy places marked by a building or altar

**silt** Particles of sand, soil, and mud carried in a river and dropped by its waters elsewhere

**steppe** Large grassland area with few trees

**surburbs** Areas surrounding a city where people live

**tectonic plates** The large solid parts that join together to form Earth's crust, or surface

**time zone** A region in which the same time is used

**trade** Buying and selling goods and services

**World Heritage Site** A place that has special cultural, historical, or scientific importance

## Further INFORMATION

## BOOKS

DK. *People and Places: A Visual Encyclopedia.* DK, 2019.

Rockett, Paul. *Mapping Asia.* Crabtree Publishing, 2017.

Son, John. *Asia.* Children's Press, 2019.

## WEBSITES

**www.kids-world-travel-guide.com/asia-facts.html**
This is the Asia section of a website aimed at young people who dream of traveling.

**kids.nationalgeographic.com/explore/countries/**
Provides a starting point for facts and photos linked to individual Asian countries and others around the world.

**www.dkfindout.com/us/earth/continents/asia**
Check out this interactive map of Asia with links to information about its geography and wildlife.

# INDEX

## ABOUT THE AUTHOR

**Mary Auld** is a writer and editor of children's nonfiction books with many years' experience. She loves introducing new ideas and perspectives to children. She has been made an Honorary Fellow of the English Association in the UK in recognition of her work.